JADE
and the Blessed Mysteries of Life

First published in France 1991.

First english edition in Canada by Alexandre Stanké, 2000.

ISBN 2-909403-54-8

Original text & illustrations: François Garagnon
Translation: James G. Anderson
Layouts: François Garagnon

www.montecristo-editions.com

First printing: first quarter 2009

PRINTED IN FRANCE

FRANÇOIS GARAGNON

JADE and the Blessed Mysteries of Life

With illustrations by the author
Translated from the French by James G. Anderson

Monte-Cristo

To God.

To Céline
To the vivacious little spirits Eloïse and Siffreine, whom one would invent if they didn't already exist.
To Sophie, Florence ("Gloria"), Isabel, Silvana and Violaine.
To Jouchka

To all the little girl-flowers who have ravished from Creation the oh so pure and delicate essence of beauty.

...And to all the grown-ups who have still within enough childhood and tenderness to marvel at it all.

The little girl whom I met is indeed a singular creature. She has gotten it into her head that it is necessary to change the essence of the world. Neither more, nor less. She plays with ideas as others play dice, but with a unique theory of probability, which, according to her, begins with a capital G...

God, of course – because it is God we are talking about –, God who seems to be having a devishily good time using the picturesque and naive mouth of this child as a vehicle for stories and parables "so important, I swear, that the future of humanity depends on them".

Her speech is a very bizarre mixture of childish naivety and moralistic wisdom, and this fusion of two such opposite styles – the one strangely questioning and the other awfully funny – produces many irresistible expressions. Their comic nature does not lessen the value of their teachings. As Jade says (and she has always the last word), for paradoxical as it may seem, it is possible to be airy and profound at the same time.

In short, Jade prefers that you listen to her "one floor up". Translation: the meaning behind the words. Clearly, her jargon would occasionally benefit from the annotations of a translator or a lexicologist. For my part, I have become accustomed to her somewhat disconcerting choice of words, though without grasping all their subtleties. I am far from fluent in her language. Certain words will remain, for you and me alike, impenetrable. For example: "a word is like an apple, you have to bite into it to discover its hidden taste, its juiciness". How could one hold this natural flirtatious behaviour against her given the inventive wealth of her poetic imagery, her freshness and her spirit of wonder?

One of Jade's discoveries is that dreams only get worn out if you don't use them. In other words, one shouldn't postpone great projects by saying "We'll see later" then continuing the daily humdrum life "jogging quietly along". No, our dreams must be acted upon here and now. One must taste them with eyes that shine like children's eyes when discovering a long-awaited and desired present.

★

I hesitated a long time before publishing this book. Jade has always symbolized for me something extremely subtle, like a passing perfume that we would like to keep hidden as our private secret. And then, one day, she spoke of fire, a flame of tenderness and things like that. She said she wanted to be, not a woman, but a flame. She had heard somewhere, I know not where, the expression "heart and soul" and she had firmly decided to be both for real, that is, precisely, the heart and the soul.

Wait... if I recall properly, it is a lot more precise than that. And if I listened with particular care, it seemed that she was trying to convey a particularly important message: she was speaking of a flame, but not like other flames, a flame at the same time very small and fragile and that, although exposed to wind, would never go out, would not stop dancing, to give warmth, light and joy to all those that came near. And she wanted us to watch her like a fire in a hearth, a fire not vowed to consume but to illuminate. At the bottom of the hearth, to the very depths of the heart. She added, as if to justify herself, "I want to be the sentimental bearer of hope…"

And thus was born the project to make Jade known to the wide world. Neither more, nor less – to use her familiar expression.

★

Paying tribute to a little girl? So what! For me, this little girl is an authentic lady! And her rule of savoir-vivre is not to avoid putting one's elbows on the table. It is to learn to stand straight. Understand: a straight spirit. To be fully worthy of taking part in the feast of life.

When I decided to tell Jade that I was writing a book about her – or more precisely about her essential remarks – I must admit that I was not quite sure how she would take it. Shall I tell you? She gave me a disdainful look, placed her hands decidedly on her hips and considered me with a touch of pity and tenderness as if I were a helpless case. “You’re crazy. They won’t understand a thing! All that was just a trilogue between you, me and God!”

She told me all that with a joking ingenuousness, which was a little short of saying sorry to have taken so much room in my heart.

I can still hear her rebelliously light laugh fly off like a kite into the great blue make-believe.

1. A Blessed Mystery

A mystery soa-
red aloft for a long time in my head before coming to rest on a branch of my conscience. It was really big and so I approached it carefully, at first because I didn't want it to fly away and, well, also because I was a little scared. This mystery was the existence of God.

I simply didn't understand why I couldn't see God anywhere when he was supposedly everywhere. One day I woke up all sunny and happy. I don't know why, but sometimes I have so much blue sky in me that I feel that I've eaten a slice of infinity. It makes your heart foam and goes to your head and you feel all bubbly inside. It's like when you've had a little too much champagne. You just stumble around happy. It's exciting, sweet and delightful!

Do you know what the Greeks called this bubbly feeling? ENTHUSIASM. Which apparently means "the exaltation produced by divine inspiration". It's the inner God. We hardly pay any attention to him because he is so discreet, and too often there is a boaster inside us who cuts him off. This is the SELF.

So there I was, drunk with happiness, and I noticed that there was no reason for this euphoria. If there is no reason, I thought, then maybe there is passion. And that's when I heard "I love you". I almost fell over! I didn't just hear this *I love you.* I felt it with my soul, my heart and my whole body. It was an infinite sea of tenderness that rose from within to immerse me. I felt like an island emerging from the ocean, all sprayed with happiness. I then understood that it was God who had submerged and subjugated me. It was from then on that a great love story began between him and me.

Since I've known God, I've changed a lot. Oh, from the outside I've only grown a few inches, but I've populated my inner kingdom with thousands of subjects of interest and I don't intend to stop there! No way! Before, I was just a little, unimportant girl. Now I'm a unique being among thousands and thousands. And it's a change that is available to everyone, on one condition: to love and feel loved. For real and for always.

God makes me so happy that sometimes I would like to have him all to myself, like a fiancé. But I can't understand that he doesn't belong to anybody but to everybody. He's both public and private, impersonal and intimate, invisible and present. But I think it's better that way. If he were too present, that would just cause problems and make people jealous. There would be insinuations and mutterings, tears and grinding of teeth, splits and divorces and maybe even lost illusions. In the end nobody would believe in him anymore. But the way it is, you see, he never forces his way into your heart. You can mope and ignore him one day and he won't hold it against you the next. He's really a neat guy when it comes right down to it. He's there not only when he wants to be, but when you need him, even at the worst of times. That's rare! When he says "I love you", he's not just moving his lips. It's with all his tenderness, with all the love in the world and with that special Godwink of his that makes instants eternal.

Every now and then I'd like to go over to the other side and put my foot down in the invisible world, just to see. But there's one problem. Since it's invisible, you can't see it! It's strange, but sometimes I want to cover my eyes to see something other than what you see with your eyes. Maybe the invisible world is even truer and more beautiful than the visible one! But how can you find out? Sometimes I want to go through the drawers in my head to see if they contain any important messages, sort through them and keep only what is essential, clear them out to make more space for God, so that I can fill myself with him! I want him to show me all the colours of the rainbow, I want him to abandon me to myself, I want him to pretend not to exist and then at the last second, when all seems lost,

I want him to come and whisper in my ear, “don’t worry Jade, I’m here! I just wanted to see if you really loved me...”

2.
Interior Landscapes

God…it's difficult to explain… He doesn't look like anybody you know, you don't hear him with your ears and you don't see him with your eyes. You feel him, that's all. I don't know if you've already met him, but it's like a magic trick. It seems so easy and yet there's always a mystery involved like an invisible bird in an unknown space.They call this invisible bird the Spirit, and sometimes it's so pure that they call it the Holy Spirit. When it flies over the countryside, the countryside becomes beautiful and luminous. When it flies over a person, the person is immediately enlightened. This Holy Spirit is like a lamplighter who lights up everything he comes near. It's easy to recognize his presence, because you breathe in a feeling of harmony, equilibrium and transparence just like a perfume. It's simple, a partnership between your little seed of life and the great garden of the infinite, between the visible and the invisible, as if the Holy Spirit were to shake your hand:

'How's it going?'

'Oh, not bad. And you?'

But that's obviously a stupid question. You don't ask the Holy Spirit how things are going, 'cause for him they're always going just fine. God's advantage is that he can make joy out of anything, even pain and suffering. I'd really like to know how he does it, 'cause some mornings I wake up with dark grey clouds in my head and I just can't get rid of them. Sometimes they even trigger terrible storms whose floodwaters overflow out of my eyes. That's when my mum comes to dry my tears with her big tender sun.

'What's the problem darling?'

I'd like to tell her, because you don't hide anything from your mother, but I don't know what to say. It's raining in my heart and I don't even know why! It just comes over me sometimes, all alone, as if I were all bent up inside with a wrinkled heart and scrambled egg eyes. It's like enthusiasm. You don't know where it comes from. But there's one difference. Enthusiasm is really neat because it helps you create happiness, whereas sadness is like a streak of bad weather when you think the sun has gone away forever! Mum laughs when I tell her about my dark grey clouds. I don't know how she does it, but mum is always happy. She's like someplace down south where it's always nice when everywhere else it's raining. When she talks to me, I see only blue sky and in no time at all she has painted everything with happy colours. She just lets the brush do the work.

'We all have rainy days', she says, 'but they don't change the landscape. Look out the window. Do you see the countryside? Of course not, because it's night, but tomorrow it will be bathed in light. Then autumn will come, then snow, then flowers will bloom again and finally the sum-

mer's heat will return. What will have changed? Everything and yet nothing. Well, our interior landscape is somewhat the same. The weather changes, there are different pressure zones, the seasons follow one another, there are cycles and rhythms, rain and nice weather. It's a perpetual metamorphosis that changes nothing. It's always the same landscape. You're always you. You have to accept yourself whether it's sunny or snowing inside.'

The good thing about mum is that she learns to contemplate beauty even if there is none ; and so I have a sort of idea that one person is a little like a landscape. If you really love him, you shouldn't expect him to be always at his best.

One day I was walking around under a little dark grey cloud. It was funny, because I had the impression that it was following me like a kite attached to me by an invisible string. Naturally, after a little while, I got used to my little grey cloud and began to like it and find it beautiful. You see things differently when you discover their beauty. That's when I realized that one side of the dark grey cloud is always lit up by the sun.

It's raining underneath, but on top it's always nice.

Well, I guess that's the advantage of the Kingdom of Heaven: guaranteed sunshine year round!

With us it's the same. Our spirits remain high if they are turned upwards, towards the good Lord. If we are able to concentrate on the upside of the inside, we will never be turned inside out or upside down. Get it?

You know, I've already known unhappiness and I've discovered that the only way to clear away the fog within is with smileshine. I know that you'll say that it's hard to smile when you're unhappy, but you can learn. And you'll soon notice that it's much harder to be unhappy when you're smiling. That's for sure!

2.

The Parable of the Two Sentinels

One day mum told me a story. I don't know if it was true, perhaps it was a children's story, but in any case it was so beautiful that it made me cry. That didn't make mom too happy, though, 'cause she told me this story on purpose to try and get rid of my dark grey clouds. I told her that they were tears of joy. She no doubt thought I was just saying that to please her, but really it was true.

So, it was at night and I wanted her to tell me a story with her big tender sun, and here's what she told me.

"When I was a little girl I was convinced that there were celestial employees whose job was to make it rain or shine. The weather, therefore, depended on their moods. When they were feeling gloomy or even downright rotten, they would program rain for a prolonged period. At other times their extravagance consisted of abundant rays of August sunshine in mid-winter, cold fronts and mountain-top snowfalls in spring, or violent thunderstorms in the heat of the summer with Jupiter-like thunder, apocalyptic fireworks and evil storms. On earth, nobody understood a thing and the weathermen tried to maintain their credibility by talking about high and low pressure zones...

"This image of employees in Heaven inspired another. Our state of mind is what determines our inner climate. When the weather patterns of our heart are stable, we have a permanent smile and we feel happy and luminous. On the other hand, when our weather vane is out of kilter, we can only expect tears and grinding of teeth. With a little practice, though, we are free to influence our inner climate at will.

"All, in the end, depends on our state of mind. Self-confidence breeds success, illusions create deception, systematic fear brings failure and love inspires hope... All of the events that we experience find their roots in our conscious and subconscious inclinations.

"I'm going to tell you a story about our inner climates. It's already a little late and I hope you're ready to abandon yourself to the sweetness of dreams with the wonderment of my little Jade who listen so carefully to stories. Are you ready, my little princess?

"Here is *The Parable of the Two Sentinels*.

"Once upon a time there was an immensely rich and powerful Prince who lived in a far-off land. One day he decided to go in search of the one thing that he did not have, happiness.

“He began by fixing the needle of his barometer on fair and immobilizing his weather vane, because when it was out of kilter, he was too. Indeed, he had noticed how sensitive is man’s state of mind – those inner climates which regulate our happiness or our misery – and so he had decided to take no chances.

“Next he recruted two oracles who were reputed to be the most talented in the kingdom, one for his spontaneous inspiration and the other for his wisdom and the clarity of his prophecies. The two oracles arrived on the appointed day and the Prince welcomed them into his inner sanctum.

‘My name is *Hope’*, proclaimed happily the first, and his dynamic appearance gave the Prince reason to believe that he had before him an enlightened soul.

‘My name is *Fear’*, said the other with a tremble, and his haggard eyes showed signs of anxiety.

“As soon as the Prince saw them, he was surprised to see how different the oracles were, and his surprise grew when he learned that this odd pair were first cousins who never left each other’s sight.

‘Why are you so radiant?’ he said to the one.

‘Because I am hope’, answered he as if evident.

‘And why are you so ashen-faced?’ he said to the other.

‘I take after my mother, whose name is also fear’.

“The Prince dubbed his two oracles *Makers of the Royal State of Mind* and ordained that they should be his devoted sentinels to keep watch over his feelings both day and night. They were to scan the horizons and notify him as soon as any telltale signs appeared in the sky. They regularly produced inner weather reports, which governed the state of mind of their Prince. In short, they made it rain or shine in the heart of their master.

“For the Prince, each new day brought the agony of waiting, for his sentinels provided him with contradictory information that invariably confused him so that he knew neither whom to trust nor where to turn. For the same event, one sentinel would encourage his hopes and stoke his dreams of peace and happiness, while the other continually contaminated him with doubt and the virus of indecision.

"Hope would ardently say, 'Look how nice it is out! See how everything under the sun is both simple and sublime! What are you waiting for to be happy? Life is like a mother holding out her arms to you. I am going to convert your heart to enthusiasm and fervour'.

"Fear, on the other hand, saw it as his duty to temper the excessive lyrical outbursts of his cousin by taking the Prince aside and exposing to him all the probable evils lurking behind these momentarily clear skies. He would gravely whisper in his ear, as a confidant honouring him with an important secret, 'Sure, it's nice out now, but it won't last. When all seems rosy, watch out! There's always something hidden. Nothing is eternal under the heavens and what is today may very well not be tomorrow. Nature is a cruel mistress'.

"Thus torn between Hope and Fear, the Prince felt a profound uneasiness, which was all the more intense since he had fallen in love with a young beauty the simple thought of whom alternately caused in him intense feelings of joy and strange bouts of doubt and painful torment.

"The day a violent storm broke out in the heart of the Prince, Fear said to him with victory in his voice, 'I told you so! See, I'm always right'.

"The Prince immediately sent for Hope and asked him with as much spite as severity, 'Why did you lie to me?'

"Hope smiled. 'Man of little faith! As the storm comes after the thunder, so the pure and luminous sky succeeds the storm and the landscape is bathed anew. You must simply wait for the end of the storm. If you shut yourself in at home for fear of the rain, then the seasons will monotonously pass by and you will take shelter from the most wonderful offerings of nature, which, in the human soul, are called passions. And you will die without having truly savoured the raging night storm which ushers in the beauty of the following day and the delicious caress of a newly heated sun'.

'Don't listen to him,' answered Fear. 'Life is an ever crying fountain'.

"Hope corrected, 'life is an ever singing fountain. The secret is in the listening'.

'Fear', thought the Prince, 'rhymes with tear,

but Hope stands alone, like childhood'. The Prince decided to give Fear less credit in the future.

'What good is too much wisdom', he thought, 'if it only leads to worries about tomorrow and perpetual fear of untoward happenings? Perhaps the best things in life come to an end, but they have a beginning too. So let's start to be happy and a little less sensitive to the weight of things, whose nature it is to disturb the horizons and to overshadow for a while, and only a while, our enthusiasm. What does it matter if the sun is but a fleeting and pitiful challenge to the elements, provided that we are able to appreciate its caress and taste its kiss. And if the cycle of the seasons renders the sun less warm and more

scarce, let us consider that it is but her flirtatious nature. From what well would we draw the overwhelming joy of renewed acquaintances if it were not from that of separation?'

"And so the Prince of this far off land, who had previously wanted to rule over all, including the secret garden of each of his subjects, decided to abandon himself to the changing winds.

"He set free his weather vane as well as the needle of his barometer. The former had quite some difficulty in deciding between the courtship of the four winds. That very evening it married a south-easterly and the Prince closed his shutters with a smile of satisfaction. Several hours later he seemed to hear between two dreams the voice of the west wind. But, as if to convince himself that there would be no unexpected turn, he abandoned himself to fate and went back to sleep with the image of the weather vane flirting with the southern wind.

"The next morning the Prince began his first day of true happiness. All was gloomy and dark around him and under the heavens, but his heart was stable. He had decided to take Hope on full-time and to name him the lone sentinel of the Royal State of Mind. Fear left with a sigh, but had little trouble finding another position, for, despite his bad reputation, he was very sought after by men. ”

4.
The Force of Abandon

At school my teacher keeps telling me, "Jade, if you want to, you can... To want is to be able..." and all sorts of variations on the same theme. Well, I'm going to tell you something. She's got it all wrong!

I'm not saying that to annoy her, 'cause I like her a lot, she's nice – a little simple-minded sometimes, but no more than other grown-ups. She's wrong, because what's important in life is not will, but abandon. I knew that would make you smile... You're thinking, that's it, Jade has invented the hammock philosophy with feet up and toes fanned out! But do you seriously think that's what I'm like? When I say *abandon*, that doesn't mean that you sit around twiddling your thumbs waiting for something to happen. That's more like being chicken or giving up or just not caring. I'm talking about abandoning yourself to the divine will. It's simple. Rather than counting on my little personal will, I rely on God's will. I noticed that he does things much better than I can. He's the best, you know! Only, he doesn't like lazy people. You have to give him a hand. You have to *believe!* What's important is to have faith. That's why I think that my teacher should say, "If you believe, you can". That would be real advice. For a lifetime.

It's a great find, abandon yourself to God's will. The problem is that people no longer believe in it. They only believe in themselves and so they just act according to their own desires, which, of course just doesn't work, or not for very long, anyway. And since it doesn't work they say that life is a raw deal. Now that's serious, because life is a great love story and people miss out because they don't love enough. They don't dare to love, or they love poorly. It's not that they don't love God, they just don't think about him, or they don't dare to think about him, because they don't really trust him.

They just want God to leave them alone. Each to his own. So then God doesn't insist. He'll come in if you leave the door open, or a little ajar, or even when the door is closed if he sees a little light underneath. But if you lock your heart shut and want to stay in the dark, he will not try to force his way in. It's not that he couldn't do it, you know, 'cause God is all powerful. He could be a heartbreaker anytime he wanted, but he prefers not to. He leaves man free to choose. And since people have loads of problems, conscious and subconscious, they choose solitude and they shut themselves up inside and it's kind of like a big desert where nothing ever happens, nothing but lost illusions. Well of course, 'cause they've left out the great Lord! You don't see their loneliness from the outside, because there are people all around, but that doesn't mean a thing. So long as you don't have God within, you are like an empty shell, all alone, completely alone.

It's my dark grey clouds that made me understand all that. It's funny, you know, but when we say "It's nice out" or "It's raining out", we don't stop to think why. It's God, though. He's the one who makes it rain or shine. Well, it's the same inside you, you're the one who makes the weather. In the morning you can decide, "Well, enough tears, today it'll be nice!" All you have to do is say it. You can get help too if you want. For example, when you're extra sad and it's raining really hard in your heart, if you think about God and smile just a little, do you know what he'll do? He'll take that little smile, add some sun and light you up from within. The smile is like a wink to God, so it's normal that it produces miracles. The dark grey clouds disappear as if by magic into the great blue of eternal harmony.

It's kind of like mum with her big tender sun. Sometimes I'm so unhappy that I think the sun has gone away forever and that God no longer lives at the same address. If I follow the advice of my teacher – "Jade, if you want to, you can" – it's no go, I can't change my thoughts. But when mum's there, I let myself go, because I love her so very, very much, sometimes even more than God, 'cause she can hold me in her arms and I feel like a little bird in a warm nest and it's great. Then the sun comes back, because I abandon myself to mummy and her tenderness, which is like God's will, 'cause God only wants true tenderness in our lives. Get it?

But abandon isn't only for when it's crying in your heart, it's for every day. Take plans for example. We all have plans and we all want them to succeed, but too often we go about it the wrong way. We want so much that we wear ourselves out by expending too much energy. And what's more is that things never go according to plan. So why plan? You might as well just let yourself go! But beware, letting yourself go doesn't mean that you just wait for something to happen. It's much more subtle than that! Here, I'll explain.

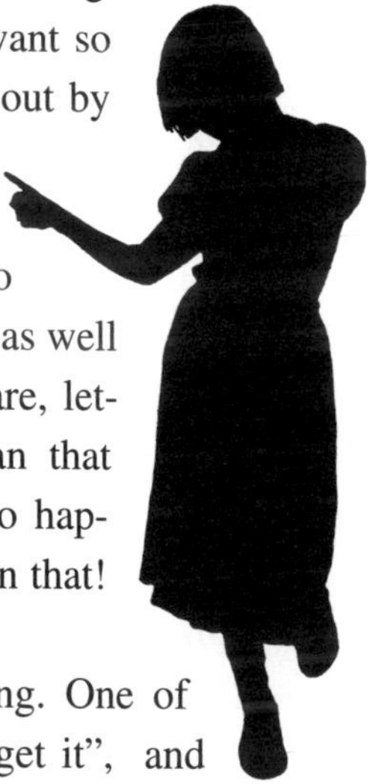

Two people want something. One of them says, "I want it, so I'll get it", and everybody applauds, because their teachers used to tell them, "If you want to, you can". So everyone says "That guy is a fighter, he'll go far". But you know, he'll never get anywhere! It's like Napoleon said. People who know where they're going don't go very far. The other guy, though, he's not really sure where he's going, but he has a general idea and he's really enthusiastic, and even more important, he knows the secret of abandon. So he just abandons himself and everything else falls into place. He's like an athlete. At a given moment he just lets the rhythm of the game take over, 'cause it's the rhythm that's going to win it for him, not his will. Take a surfer, for example. If you watch carefully, you'll notice that he does his best when he goes with the wave, but if he tries to fight it, he's guaranteed to fall. He's got to let his instinct take over and stop trying to reason the wave. It's intuition and feeling. For us it's the same. When we're surfing on a sea of mystery, we have to learn to abandon ourselves to the rhythm of the wave. It's the only way to keep our balance and not get tumbled over and our nose ground into the beach!

When you abandon yourself, you liberate your best qualities. All that was shut up is set free and you open yourself up to life and you feel delivered of a burden. It's the power from within that will overcome all obstacles, like a rushing river that nothing can stop and that feeds itself. Abandon brings abundance, perpetual abundance. If you simply rely on your will, it's like opening the tap just a little to let out a trickle of energy. By trying to save, your heart is threatened by drought and nothing will grow there, neither success, nor plans, nor tenderness, nor anything worth living for.

I've got a big secret to tell you... come here, I'll whisper it in your ear... Where there's abandon, there's love and where there's love, there's God. It's a fact! You have to make a choice then give your all without holding back, abandon yourself to the current when you know that the source is pure and just let yourself be carried along, feel the rhythm and the harmony, savour the taste of life and thank God with a big tender sun for guiding us towards unknown worlds without getting tired or bored, without slowing down, far far far away. Let God flow within you like a river. That's all. When you've understood, you'll see, life just flows naturally along…

5.
Open Up the Spring

We all have to become springs where people want to come and quench their thirst.

Have you noticed how we don't say, "I'm dying of hope", but rather, "I'm dying of thirst". That's proof enough that thirst is really important, 'cause our lives depend on it. There are a lot of people who go on living without realizing that they are dead. I mean, they exist, but they don't really live. Living isn't just breathing, moving, getting up, working and going to the bank to get money! Do you think that you'll remember all that at the end of your life? It'll all be a big jumble and there won't be anything worth remembering, and anyway you'll probably be senile and mix everything up! Even though you will have lived billions and billions of instants, it will be like nothing has really happened. And you'll say, "So that's life, huh?" and it'll be as if you hadn't even seen it go by.

Is that how you want to end up? Hey, I'm sure you've got lots of plans stored up in your head, right? Well, of course, there are plans and then there are plans. There's what you want to have, but then that's your business. What's much more interesting is what you want to *be*. You often think of what you have always wanted to do. It's just that you find all kinds of excuses for not doing it, things out of your control, no time, the necessities of daily life... So you say, "I'll do it later". But what does "later" mean? You really want me to tell you? Later means never!

If you want to do it and you don't, what good is it to be able to do it? You're no better off than the guy who can't do it! You're even worse off, because it's not the fault of the guy who can't do it, but you, you're wasting your talent. It's as if you're happy and don't show it. How can anyone know you're happy? You might as well not be! Anyway, happiness is so great and so abundant that you can't just keep it all for yourself, otherwise it's not 100 per cent prime happiness. It's a mixture of pleasure, selfishness and excitement, a tra la la and not an *alleluia*.

I'm going to tell you something. Dreams only get worn out if you don't use them! If you wait for your dreams to collect dust, you'll soon be an old scarecrow full of cobwebs. If you don't carry out your plans now, it's because they're full of hot air, or else you're chicken. You have to make a choice. Either you raise yourself up to the level of your dreams or you remain where you are, a little uninteresting guy nailed to the ground all his life because he supposedly doesn't have time to gaze at the stars... That's the way it is!

Do you know why people don't dare? It's because they've reduced their lives to a trickle of water. They're afraid of failing and so they open the tap slowly... drip drip drip. They're saving up, you see!

I have a friend named Raphael and he's not a trickle, he's a waterfall. One day I asked him where he got all his energy from and if he wasn't afraid to run dry by giving too much of himself. He laughed like crazy, but not to make fun of me, 'cause at times like those he says that I'm "quite a little darling". He said to me, "Jade, really, you're irresistible", and then he told me all.

"Have you ever really looked at a waterfall? It's like a never ending fall and rebirth. The water never stops falling and you'd even say that the faster it flows away the faster it comes. The more energy it spends the more generous it seems, and the more impulsive it becomes, the more pure it is! Well, you're the same.

"Have you ever heard of the water table? It's the underground water that feeds wells and springs. Well, I think that we have water tables throughout our whole bodies. If there is no outlet for them then the water tables dry up and so does your heart. That's why we have to become springs for others. So they don't die of thirst. Of course you don't just say you're a spring, you become one. Perhaps you think that you have to get a lot of water to give some away. You're wrong! Mr. Saint Exupéry once said, "the more you give, the more you enrich yourself; the more you go to the true spring, the more generous it becomes". Do you understand?"

I have to admit that it wasn't easy to understand. To sum up Raff's thoughts: the more you do for free, the richer you get. OK! Do you think a shopkeeper will take me seriously when I tell him, "the more you give, the richer you get"? He'll burst out laughing and say, "Look, you're a nice girl, but you won't work at my checkout counter".

I thought about it a lot and decided that it wasn't a question of money, but of heart. Sure, you can do things for your own pleasure, but the greatest pleasure comes from giving pleasure. For the pleasure of God! *Gratis pro Deo*! Raff calls that "sublime giving". He says, "What's the use of hoarding your heart? Feelings that you don't give are lost feelings!" When you've understood that, you no longer give drop by drop, you give in torrents. The more you open your spring, the faster the water flows! The more you give, the richer you get! Wow, if I could get rich like that!.. Do I dare? It would be great to be a billionaire in feelings!

6.

Carpe Diem

Last night I couldn't get to sleep. A mystery was gliding to and fro in my head and it was making me quite dizzy. I guess I should say that it was a big, big mystery, almost as big as the one about the existence of God. I even thought that it might be the same strange bird as before.

Fate and destiny... I'd already talked about these subjects a lot with mum, but these talks just brought up more and more important questions, so important, I swear, that the future of humanity depends on them. I was born by chance, I met Raff by chance, everything important that has happened in my life has been "by chance". And the problem is that we don't know anything about chance. These ideas were trotting about in my head, pacing back and forth, and I ended up waking up my mum.

'Mum, who's chance?'

'What's the matter, Jade, did you have a nightmare?'

'No. I can't get to sleep so long as I don't know who chance is. Tell me.'

'C'mon now, Jade, chance isn't Father Christmas! Perhaps you'd like me to tell you that it's me?'

'If it's you, tell me it's you! But I have my own opinion on the question... Chance is God, right? It's God's will. He's the one behind all this! So why doesn't he admit it?'

Mum heaved a long sigh and I was sorry that I'd woken her up, but it was stronger than me. I absolutely had to know. She told me:

'God created man to be free. He doesn't want to seem to meddle in what's none of his business... so perhaps he just meets men somewhere along the road of life, by chance, we say, or by coincidence.'

'But I'm not free if he forces me to submit to

his will! Anyway, I've heard about predestination. I don't do what I want to do, I do what he wants me to do. I'm nothing but a puppet.'

'Do you think that God wants us to be evil? Do you think he wants men to go to war? Do you think he wants them to hate, betray and kill each other?'

'Oh no, I don't believe that because, by definition, God wants everbody to love each another. But...'

'So that proves that men surely do as they please! You know, Jade, these are big questions that you're asking me. You can't answer them just like that, because afterwards you'll have preconceived notions and be mistaken for the rest of your life'.

'What's your opinion?'

'Goethe said: "In life the cards are dealt, but with a given hand, each person can play the game differently". In other words, in the game of life we all have cards, trumps, but the outcome of the hand will depend on us, our talent, our ability to adapt and the brilliance with which we master the instant as a function of the whole. There are those who squander their trumps, just as there are others who win even though they begin with serious handicaps. Nothing is ever a foregone conclusion.

"In the Bible there is a fundamental question: "What have you done with your talent?" which proves that God has left man free to conduct his life as he wishes. God planted the seeds for man to cultivate and care for. Each man is free to make them grow or let them die! That is why there are many seeds which will never blossom. That is man's freedom, the power to say yes or no, to tend or to ignore, to bring to fruition or to trample underfoot'.

'So you're saying that we have unlimited freedom?'

'Not exactly... let's call it an unlimited liberty in the limited framework of our destiny. You are born in the middle of a field of possibilities, with certain talents. You can't do everything, there are even things that you will never be able to do. But there are many other things that you can do and it's up to you to choose from among these possibilities and use your talent to the fullest. Do you understand?'

The next day I was in such a hurry to see Raff

to talk to him about chance and destiny that I arrived all out of breath.

'Tell me Raff... have you already cultivated... possibilities?'

'What? What are you talking about?'

'Possibilities. It seems I was born in the middle of a field of possibilities…'

Raff laughed like crazy. He sat down, took me by the arm, and said, "You know, you're quite a little darling you are! A field of possibilities isn't like a field of beans, tomatoes or potatoes! Your field of possibilities is the area of your freedom, the space where you can make your wishes become reality, in short, where things are accessible to you, where possibilities are offered".

He's smart, Raff! He always has an answer to everything. I told him all that mum had said and then I asked him his advice. He got up, made a gesture as if to show me all the expanse of the sky and said: "*Carpe diem*".

'What?'

'*Carpe diem.* What do you think that means?'

'I dunno... a kind of car?'

That really made him laugh!

'You're getting warm, my little princess! It's got something to do with the highway code. It's a path, if you will, a code of conduct in life.'

He got serious again, took me by the arm and I plunged my eyes into his blue eyes, so deeply

that I thought I was going to drown.

'Listen to me carefully and try to remember all that I'm about to say, because it's very, very important. *Carpe diem* in Latin means, "make the most of the present day". Horace is the one who said this to remind people that life is short and fleeting and that you must not waste it. Most people don't know how to make use of their time. They're always saying, "I don't have the time. I've got too much to do..." That's the worst of arguments and people use it all their lives, as if it were a legitimate excuse! Remember this well: you don't have time to waste your time. Life is too short to live it halfway. You must live the hours of your existence to their fullest extent. They won't all be intense, of course, because life is made of contrasts, but you can't deny any of them. Most lives are made up of lamentations, regrets and lost illusions. People say, "If I'd only had the time, I would have done such and such" or "If I'd only been able to do that. Well, you can't always do what you want in life, you have to make do with reality", and all sorts of other garbage of the same kind! I'm telling you to dream, Jade, dream! Not for the pleasure of dreaming, but to go to the end of your dreams! Each one of us holds the end of a piece of string with which we can tie the knot of truth.

"Do you know how many seconds there are in one day? Eighty-six thousand four hundred! Each day you live eighty-six thousand four hundred seconds, do you realize? That's a hell of a stockpile, eh? You can do thousands of things with that kind of time!'

I couldn't get over it. I never would have believed that there could be so many seconds in one little day! I got out a piece of paper and a pencil and did a calculation, and do you know what? I figured out that a baby, just twelve days after arriving on earth, is already a millionaire... in seconds! Then I asked myself what I did with all of these billions and billions of seconds? Some people say time is money, but I hope they're wrong, 'cause imagine all the debts we'd have! With all the time we waste, we'd have billions and billions of debts! So, why don't we live our lives better? Tell me Raff, what's the meaning of life?

"The meaning of life? Here's the secret. Do your best, then let God do the rest. Don't listen to those who want to distance you from your dreams, those who want to discourage you along the way, those who no longer believe. What do they know about your mystery? It's up to you to express it fully, with all the strength of your love. You have to be crazy in love with life! You must dare to take chances! Even when you think you're being daring, you're not being daring enough. Remember that when you give of yourself, it's never "too much", it's always "not enough". You can never love too much. You can make a mistake, you can love badly, but you can never love enough. Never, you hear!

"Do your best, Jade. You know, we do evil so well and we do good so poorly. That's it, do your best! And when you've done everything you possibly can, don't forget to let go and abandon yourself to God's will, because if you don't have faith, true faith, well, your dreams will be blown away like dead leaves by the autumn wind.

"One day God will come and visit your inner garden and he will ask you, *What have you done with your talent?* It would be good to be able to turn around with a big smile and show him all that you've done in your life with love. "Here you are, My Lord". God will see all of the little seeds that you have planted and cared for and that have become shoots, trees, flowers and fruits. Then he will turn to you and I am willing to bet that he'll also say, *you're quite a little darling, Jade !*"

7.
The Spirit of Wonder

I really want to amaze God. It's true that I'd like him to admire me and tell me that I'm "irresistible" and to give me a cuddle from time to time! I have a secret code with Raphael with lots of words in foreign languages like Greek and Latin and Hebrew, so that no one can understand, just us two and God. Our three main passwords are *Carpe Diem, Alleluia* and *Eureka.* These are key words which fit into all of life's locks; they open all doors, all of them!

Carpe Diem-Alleluia-Eureka! These three words form our philosophy. Shall I translate them for you? Well, first, you have to know how to make the best use of the present day (that's

Carpe Diem). Second, you need to be full of joy to thank God for the life he has given you (*Alleluia!*) And third, you need to spend your time looking for solutions of hope, tirelessly, until you find them (*Eureka*). With this philosophy, like Raff says, you can really live your dream instead of spending all your time dreaming your life!

I met Raphael by accident one day on a hill where he had just landed. I didn't tell you, did I? He flies. No, he's neither a bird nor an angel and he hasn't got wings. He's simply the pilot of a small plane. He makes regular flights over land and sea. He has baptized his flying machine *Spirit of Wonder*.

"It carries its name well", he tells everyone. "It starts right up, lets you see things like you've never seen before, and what's more, it never breaks down."

I'm telling you, Raff could have been a travel agent! The only problem is that people don't dare get in his plane. After all, it's not very solid any more, 'cause he's had to repare it all over and it has been rusted by salt water and deformed by his acrobatics.

Raff has really been around, you know. He's seen all the colors of the rainbow, and I have to tell you that he knows what he's talking about. He's told me lots about what he's seen. For example, in certain countries, it seems that churches are open all day and all night and people can go in and out as they please. There are a lot of old people who come and pray, maybe because they're afraid of death. And there are a lot of young people too, maybe because they're afraid of life. In any case, those people, old and young, feel like they don't amount too much if God doesn't give them a hand, so they go to church to pray a little just like others go to a bar to drink a little. The difference is that they do it to remember, and the others to forget. It's a fact!

According to Raphael there's one quality that allows you to obtain everything and to make your dreams come true, to live a great love, never to despair, to always adore God and even to fly up into the infinite blue yonder. Just one quality needed to do all that! Raff says it's the most important quality in the world, the best one that a person can ever have. It's the SPIRIT OF WONDER! *Carpe Diem-Alleluia-Eureka*. They're no good without the Spirit of wonder. You might as well try and fly without wings!

"*Spirit of Wonder*" is the name of Raff's plane. He says, "The day *the Spirit of Wonder* crashes will be the end of the world!"

When I see him take off in his old crate with propellers, it sends shivers up and down my spine. First because Raphael is an old friend, but also because I wonder if the world really will come to an end the day that the "*Spirit of Wonder*" folds up its wings...

Raphael has divided the world of men into two categories, the *what's-the-users* and the *why-notters*. For him there are those who say "What's the use?" and who only see the obstacles to overcome, and then there are those who say "Why not?" and who only see the goal to attain. What makes him sad is that there are more and more *what's-the-users* and those guys are killers. They kill the spirit of wonder. They get some kind of weird pleasure out of criticizing everything and complaining about everything, and they give up at the first opportunity. They're bored and they go through life as if nothing really had any importance. Raphael calls them "background people", because they are creatures who have lost all contact with Creation. One day Raff gave me a *Carpe Diem-Alleluia-Eureka* sermon that I am not about to forget. Here's what he said:

"Don't let yourself be taken in by them, Jade, you deserve much more than that. Don't be so foolish as to want to resemble those around you! When you wake up in the morning, be aware that there is no certainty that you will be alive when the sun sets. Isn't that the best of reasons to say "thank you" every day to He-who-powers-the-universe-and-regulates-all-things for having made the earth so beautiful? Isn't that a reason for marvelling at life in any way, shape or form down to the imperceptible shivering of the grass in the evening breeze? Isn't that a reason to be on the lookout for great occasions, people of value and all that is worthy of hope? Isn't that a reason to live fully your joys and to bravely endure your hardships?

"Never forget to inhale the fragrance of life, to feed the flame of inner elation, to be sensitive to the caress of the air as you pass through it and to fill all of your senses with the images, smells and melodies of the world. Yes, never forget to savour the taste of life, its royal nectar gathered from flowers pure, that marvellous warm honey of secret and magic virtues".

Well, after that I stood at attention before the captain of the *Spirit of Wonder* and I spoke out like an oath: "Carpe Diem-Alleluia-Eureka!"

8.
The Be-Attitudes

Raff often talks about happiness. According to him there are three Be-Attitudes. Be beautiful, be kind and be good. If your inner climate goes sour, it's certain, you have a Be-Attitude problem.

One day he wanted to start a club of happy people, the Good Mood Club. The hardest thing was to recruit. There were just two of us, whereas there were millions and millions of bad humoured people. Of course, at first the Good Mood Club draws lots of people, because it's always nice there, only it's very, very difficult. Not to get in, but to stay in.

Sometimes when you get up in the morning

you're all lit up with happiness, so much so that you shine. Then the day begins and you meet people who have dark grey clouds filing through their head. They're so threatening that you get the impression that all you'd have to do would be to poke them lightly to start a great big storm. So obviously it's not easy to remain sunny. You get discouraged after a while and you start to think that you're wasting your sunshine for nothing at all. Finally you end up going over to the other side where the people are in a bad mood. You say to yourself, "After all, there's no reason why I should try since no one else does!" It's funny. It's as if it were more fun to play the devil's advocate than the accomplice of God. There's no justice!

Raff says that bad moods are like the flu. If one person has it, ten will get it. What I don't understand is why we can't infect people with good moods too. Raff told me that diseases are much easier to transmit than the Be-Attitudes. But we all live under the same sky and that should be enough to make us reach out and smile a lot to warm up each others' hearts. My feminine intuition tells me that there's something floating in the air, a temptation, but people don't dare. They don't dare smile and I don't know why. And yet the first rule of happiness is always to have a smile.

Well, Raff and I decided to go on good mood diets. You have to fast a lot. For days and days we don't say one bad, mean or evil word and we only see what's going well. Even if we have big dark grey clouds floating around inside us we're not allowed to let them rain. All we have to do is look at their tops, you know, the side that is always facing the sun. At first it's very, very difficult, 'cause we just want to let ourselves go, but afterwards it's really neat. It's like the sun that heats you up in the middle of winter. Even if everyone else is cold, we stay warm from all the heat we've saved up during our good mood diet.

I don't know if you've noticed, but what separates people is words. Even little words that seem to mean nothing can cause the worst of evils. There are words that hurt and also words that kill. For example, Raff says that love can begin with a gesture and finish with one word too many. Maybe we dress reality with words because we are afraid to sec it naked. Maybe we should also keep quiet more often. Learn to contemplate. Say nothing. Remain silent. But not any old silence, no sir! There are

all kinds of silences, serious, shrill and intense. There is the silence which hides absence and emptiness. There is the silence because we don't dare. There is the silence, because we don't want to say anything or because we don't care. There is the silence because we close our eyes and don't want to meddle in what's none of our business. None of these are good silences. No, I'm talking about silences with stars, silen-ces shared by two, with gestures and messages and shared sculptures, silences soft and round like tenderness and intoxicating like love. A dense silence, the dance of silence...

Lovers adore nothing more than silence. It's funny. It's when they say nothing that they understand each other the best. So much so that Raff once said, "true love is when silence is no longer a void to be filled, but a harmony to be shared ". When you love someone, that someone is like God. It's someone who doesn't ressemble anyone, who doesn't need to talk to be present, who is capable of lighting up the universe with a smile and, when you think hard about him, of transporting you into a world that doesn't exist or that only exists elsewhere.

What I noticed right away about Raff is that, even when he's silent, even before he speaks, he's not like other grown-ups. Do you know many grown-ups who realize their dreams? Well Raff, he can! You know, he's not an old person, he's still a little kid!

9.
The Mysterious Ceremonial

Do you know how I met Mr. Holy Spirit for the first time? You're going to laugh and think that I'm having you on, but this is exactly the way it happened.

God has allowed me to meet some very exceptional people who have become friends. I say ' God has allowed me ', because of course you don't choose and it is God who progressively deals us the most important cards in the game of life, chance meetings. And if I say that these people are entirely exceptional, it's not because they're my friends, but because they sing fully their lives, whereas others just whisper theirs with timid lips.

Raphael, for example, is like a match. He

doesn't seem to amount too much, but he's got so much love crackling inside of him that he'd be capable of setting the whole world alight. Like I said, Raphael flies an old crate and he's always talking about some guy named Mr. Saint Exupéry, who was apparently a little prince who flew off to another planet. At first I didn't really understand how he could go to another planet like that and I thought he might be like Mr. Holy Spirit who can go everywhere. That really made Raff laugh, but then he thought about it and said, "Do you know, you're quite a phenomenon!" Well, of course I knew that, but I couldn't really see what he was getting at. And then one day he came by, picked me up off the ground and held me up towards the infinite blue yonder, right at the end of his arms and with a flame in the hearth of his eyes said to me, "I met Mr. Holy Spirit!"

I thought he was just saying that to make fun of me, but then he told me some unbelievable things that made me want to meet Mr. Holy Spirit too.

"Think about how your life has gone. Have you really chosen the important moments? No, they came all by themselves. You were acted upon. It's like enthusiasm: it goes through you, but it doesn't come from you, at least not from your will. Sometimes you spend years trying to do something with your will and nothing happens, or at least not as well as you had planned, and so you say to yourself, "I didn't deserve that. I was unlucky. Life is a raw deal!" Nevertheless, you did all you could. It's just that good will isn't active will, and active will isn't necessarily God's will. Other times you don't do anything, or at least not much, and things just happen naturally and come off without any problems. A gesture, a look or a smile can be enough to resolve everything at one stroke. On the other hand, you have perhaps noticed that sometimes when you help people, you get nothing in return for your trouble but indifference or ingratitude. Or, because you listened to somebody who needed to talk, you are warmly thanked, as if you had accomplished a miracle, but you didn't say anything, just listened. It's kind of amazing, don't you think? It isn't us or our will power that make things happen, it's our state of mind or, if you prefer, the ease with which we communicate with Mr. Holy Spirit".

At the time I didn't understand much of what Raphael said, but he was so enthusiastic about telling me that I listened carefully, and he told me that I was one of a kind (which is just as well, I think!), so I really thought about all that he had said about things happening all alone because of Mr. Holy Spirit.

One day we both went to see Amorgen, archery master. He's an old and respectable wise man and I'm just a little thing beside him, but he wants us to talk like equals, because he says that I know as much as he does, maybe even more. It's funny, but he's not a grown-up like all the others. One time I told him that he reasoned like an eight-year-old boy, and do you know what he answered? Well, he said that he was one hundred and eight years old, but that after the age of one hundred you start at zero again, so in reality he was only eight. I don't know if I should believe him, 'cause I get the impression that he's a really good joker who keeps a straight face. In any case, if he is one hundred and eight, you wouldn't know it!

So we talked about Mr. Holy Spirit and once

again Amorgen had a lot of things to teach me. He may be only eight, but he's still been around and that gives him a head start when it comes to understanding the invisible. Raphael and I spent the evening at his place and I'll never forget what I saw, 'cause I feel a hundred years wiser now. Some little girls would have preferred a bag of candy, but I swear that for me that evening was the best!

Let me tell you about it. We spent the evening talking outside and then it got very dark, so dark that we really had to open our eyes wide to see each other. Then Amorgen got up, turned his face towards the sky and said, "Here is the night, here is the silence and the wind, here is the fullness of the moment". At times like those you don't say anything, you just let him talk like he was a ghost, a poet, a prophet or a crazy man. Anyway, he's kind of like all those put together.

He said, "Jade, get two candles. Raphael, light them and place them on either side of the target which is over there. From now on it is forbidden to speak. You will not use the spoken word until the day erases the magic of this night. Fill yourselves with what you are about to see, play close attention to the ceremonial and, when it has finished, close your eyes, put your spirit at ease and meditate, my friends. Meditate the night, meditate the silence and the wind, meditate the fullness of the moment..."

This whole scene scared me a little, but I did what he asked me to. Raff and I placed the candles near the target, and I remember that it was really far away and since it was very dark out we almost missed the spot. Raphael lit the candles and we went back. Out of curiosity, I counted my steps and there were sixty-one. I never would have thought that thirty yards was so far!

When we got back, Amorgen was sitting on the ground, cross-legged Indian style. You could only make out his shape and he seemed petrified. He was more motionless than a blade of grass and that struck me, because I wondered if he was maybe over on the other side of life. Neither Raff nor I dared budge, because we sensed that something important was about to happen, but

what? We waited like that for a long time and then finally Amorgen got up slowly and took his bow. The target was practically invisible, because the wind had blown out the candles, but as our eyes got used to the dark we could barely make out a shadowy circle on the horizon. Amorgen's look was lost in this obscurity, the bow was turned towards the ground and his right hand gently stroked an arrow. And then everything happened very fast. I heard the release of an arrow, a whistling and a dull sound and Amorgen gave a little yelp. Then he fired two other arrows just as fast. It was like he wasn't even aiming. He said with a strange voice, "Something fired and struck the target". We went the sixty-one steps to see. Raff and I looked at each other as if there had been a miracle. Two arrows had hit the bull's eye and the third one had split one of the other two. We didn't dare take them out. We stayed like that a long time thinking in the dark, and then we went back. I couldn't close my eyes all night. Just think about it: he had gone right by us, within reach... I had just come in contact with Mr. Holy Spirit!

10.
Mr. Holy Spirit

The arrow within. I had just understood that one should be drawn towards a goal, like a bow, in the right direction. If you have the rhythm, the technique and the inner balance, then you attain the target, even without aiming. Amorgen says: to decipher the invisible.

I thought about this arrow thing a lot. If you can be almost certain of hitting the target without aiming, simply due to the power of the spirit, I thought, then maybe it would be possible not just for a target placed in a field, but also for goals placed in life. Amorgen told me that I was approaching the complex subject of space-time, but I didn't understand any of his explanations. Still, I continued reasoning in my little head. I thought that if Amorgen hit his target simply by visualizing his arrow in the bull's eye, then perhaps it would be possible to do the same with plans, and that's a really interesting thought. Do you realize what I'm saying? You could reach your goals every time, pfft! just like an arrow, right smack in the middle! In other words, to attain a goal, you have to begin by imagining that you've already attained it. But not just for the pleasure of dreaming, because you really see it. Granted, it's a spirit's eye view, but it's still a true projection into the future, not just a figment of your imagination, right! The next time I see my teacher, I'll tell her that in order to look at your life in the past, first you have to live it in the present and the future. She'll probably make me stay behind to review verb tenses!

In short, Amorgen's kind of a strange guy. I suspect that he's put it into Raff's head that we don't amount too much, no more important than blades of grass. He never says "I", because he claims that he doesn't act, but that he's acted upon. I've already noticed the same thing about the dark grey clouds and enthusiasm. They both come from inside, but you don't really know where. To think that it's the same for everything, though, that there's an invisible force deep inside us that acts in our place, I'm not so sure. But he is. He doesn't say, "I met", but rather, "It was given to me to meet". Sometimes it's hilarious. For example, he doesn't say, "I'm hungry", but, "The honourable stomach is sadly empty". I don't dare imagine how he excuses himself when he has an urgent need to pee!

The evening that he hit the target in the dark, he said, "Something shot". It is true that it was strange, because it didn't seem like he'd aimed. It was like the arrows left all by themselves and flew towards the goal that was there for them, like birds bearing down on their prey. Unfailingly. In fact, all of this magic is the work of Mr. Holy

Spirit. He's always there when strange things happen that you can't explain.

Mr. Holy Spirit is really quite something! He soars above things, above people and above the world. He brushes the infinitely small with his wing and then takes off towards the infinitely large. He's constantly coming and going between the here-and-now and the beyond. When you get right down to it, he's got a really interesting job. He takes it upon himself to transfer the breath of the Creator to the creature, as if it were the Olympic flame. That's sort of true too, 'cause without him nature would be inanimate, without breath nor anything very interesting to live for. It's thanks to him that things get done and that the world goes on. Everywhere he goes there are changes, bursts of enthusiasm, subtle tremblings, amazing intuitions and miracles. The fact that he's invisible suits us just fine. Men talk of chance, luck and circumstances and I imagine Mr. Holy Spirit, draped in his anonymity, taking off like a shot towards his sky blue palace in search of a new mission. Mr. Holy Spirit is like a bird: he instinctively migrates to horizons where the climate suits him. It's not nice things that attract him, nor good nor big things, but what is done with greatness, purity and beauty. All things considered, there is only one thing that counts for him... the spirit. The spirit with which one does what one does. When there is enthusiasm, hope, joie de vivre, fraternity, prayer, you can be sure that Mr. Holy Spirit is somewhere nearby! Where there's faith, there's Mr. Holy Spirit. Wherever hearts burn, wherever lights flare and wherever flames shine (in the recesses of the fireplace or deep in the eyes), Mr. Holy Spirit is present. God is the light, man is the candle and Mr. Holy Spirit is the wick. That's why if you want to see clearly, you can't lose sight of the spirit. It's no accident that to lose your head means to go crazy!

I told Amorgen that I'd like to *be acted upon* by Mr. Holy Spirit too. He smiled and I wondered if you had to wait to be a hundred to be helped by Mr. Holy Spirit. But no, even little darlings like me have the right. So, what do you have to do to meet him? Amorgen told me that you have to get into the praying mode, but for real, not to try and make your neighbour believe that you're a saint because you're kneeling

down at church. Abandon oneself completely, forget that boaster named the SELF who's always butting in everywhere and who prevents you from hearing the subtle calls of God. Forget your flesh envelope, forget the existence of the world, and fly off into the infinite blue yonder at the speed of light! My friend, all that is easy to say, but I'd like to see you do it!

Amorgen was already engaged in interplanetary travel while I was still watching blades of grass move. And that's where everything suddenly changed! By watching blades of grass move, I swear that I ended up believing that I had become a blade of grass myself. I shuddered like the billions and billions of blades of grass in the wind, I vibrated like the billions and billions of seconds in time and the breath ran through my body. I closed my eyes and I felt light, light like smoke which disappears into the air as it rises towards the sky. Where did Jade go? Puff! Up in smoke! I couldn't say how long it lasted. It was like a piece of eternity, I mean an instant out of time, a bit of a dream in parentheses in the great sentence of my life. And I understood what it is to pray.

Amorgen approached me.

'How's it going my little princess? You seem out of it!'

'...I feel...outside of my body!'

He patted my cheek and said with a smile:

'It's all right, you still seem all there.'

11.
Bite Into the Apple

Carpe Diem-Alleluia-Eureka. You'll remember, right? Oh, I know what you're thinking. No little kid who's knee-high to a grasshopper is going to give me moral lessons! Well, why not?

I've already lived billions and billions of seconds and I might know just as much as old Amorgen who has one hundred and eight years under his belt.

One time I even passed over to the other side of life. It was in a dream. I was being chased by the Devil, who wanted to make me believe that God and Co. were nothing but silliness. I accused him of unfair competition and he took it very badly. In short, I'm not quite sure what happened next, I just know that I died. That's when I woke up. I've often thought about this incident. When you die in a dream, you wake up. Of course it's normal, because you can't imagine what comes after death! What if life were just the same? Maybe life is nothing but a dream and when you die you really do wake up. For good. Into the real world.

Well anyway, who can say? We'll all see later, when we die. But that's just it! What do you think it's like, the moment when you die? When you're just a little thing like me, you have to look far, far into the future to find out. It's a long time off, like out in space. I'd like to know what you think about before dying, because if you could know that when you're born, maybe you'd live differently!

I already know that when it comes time to sum up our lives, those billions and billions of seconds that we've lived, our numerous encounters, all our acts and deeds, we'll discover that the moments that have counted the most, those that have echoed for the longest inside us, will be those that happened by accident and not those that we willed. It'll be those moments that filtered into our existence like water into the earth to fertilize our little seed of life. That's when we opened up, bloomed, flowered and bore fruit. Life then was full of flavour and we wanted to bite into it.

Which reminds me of Fred. I haven't told you about him yet. He's a great friend, almost as great as Raff, and especially because of the place he holds in my heart. Fred says that to feel good, you have to gain altitude. That's why he's always running up mountains, trying to conquer higher and higher summits. He's kind of like Raff. He's always looking to go higher. Once I asked him, "What do you think is the meaning of life?"

He gave me a big smile, scratched his head and answered: "It's so simple that there's nothing to say. Really, it's all so easy. It's kind of like with an apple. There it is, deep down in your pocket. You can feel it all round and full of juice and you can already taste it in your mouth. It has the flavour of promise. You wait for the perfect moment, you wait until you get to the top of the mountain, after all your efforts. Then you take it out of your pocket, rub it on your sleeve and make it shine in the sun. The apple exudes a smell that makes your mouth water. Now's the time, the very instant when a simple little apple sums up the flavour of life. Now, if you were in an apple orchard, it would be quite different. There you have as many apples as your little heart could desire. You can eat them until you're stuffed and you'll never understand how heavenly the taste of an apple can be. What else is there to say? It's as easy as eating an apple, and there are no words which can ever describe the flavor of the coveted apple".

I understood what Fred meant. What's important is to savour the taste of life. When you think about it, you realize what a wonderful gift it is! Really fantastic!

"The nature of the apple doesn't change, but the apple is changed by the way you look at it, taste it and feel it. Do you understand?

"The mystery of life is in your

eyes. You simply need to train them to look beyond appearances. And remember this well, that when the universe seems to darken before you, it is not because the doors are closing, but because your eyes are fleeing the light".

12.

How to Recognize Godwinks

Of course, the problem when you try to look beyond appearances is not to be fooled, but with a little practice, it's quite easy, because there are Godwinks everywhere.

First, God is everywhere where there's light. Light is invisible, right: what you see is what's lit up. Well, God's the same. He's invisible: what you see is what he lights up. As for the sun, don't worry, God knows what he's doing!

God is in the sun of the day and the moon of the night, and when there are eclipses, he discreetly appears in the dim brightness of the stars. The builders of churches and cathedrals did everything possible so that God can filter in when he wants, through the stained-glass windows, the rose windows and everywhere. But there are many other kinds of light, the sparkling of a torrent, the gold of autumn leaves, a pearly white smile, a drop of dew and mum's eyes when she looks at me with her big tender sun.

It is with your eyes that you perceive the light from without, and it is with your eyes that you express the light from within. Have you noticed, it's with your eyes that you give and you receive. As Fred says, your eyes are for looking beyond appearances.

At first I didn't really understand. When people pray to God, they say, "Deliver us from our blindness". I just didn't understand how all these people could be blind, so I asked Raphael. He told me that I was blind too.

'Well', I said, 'I beg to differ, but I see just fine thank you!'

'Not at all', he said and I got mad. I had the impression he was saying that just to get me worked up.

He went on, "Since you see so well, can you tell me the colour of the wind, where Mr. Holy Spirit is and what tomorrow will consist of? Can you tell me if the encounter you have today will change your whole life or if you'll forget it in a few days? Can you tell me what's beyond the horizon? And why you only see stars at night?"

I was flabbergasted. Of course I couldn't tell him.

'The moral', Raff said, 'is that we only see the present and visible world. The future and the invisible world escape our perception.'

'What about Amorgen, then? He deciphers the invisible doesn't he?'

'Well, yes he does, with the help of Mr. Holy Spirit. That's why he has to meditate for so long beforehand, to have a clear vision, or rather a clairvoyance. But he doesn't see with his eyes. Do you know what Mr. St. Exupéry's Little Prince used to say? "*You only see well with your heart. The essential things in life are invisible to the eyes*" '

I had just learned something vitally important. Hidden truths don't exist. Truths don't hide. It is our strange blindness that prevents us from perceiving them. Just one more reason to pay attention to Godwinks!

I guess you could say that Raff had just opened my eyes! My new discovery completely revolutionized my method of prayer. Usually when we pray, we ask God for lots of things we think we need at the time. But since we are blind, how can we know that we'll still need them later on? We make choices, pray so that they come true, and it doesn't work. So we begin to doubt our faith and say, "If God existed, there would be justice!" It's funny. As soon as we have something to hold against God, as soon as he doesn't do as we've asked, we get even by saying that he doesn't exist! You gotta be kidding! God just laughs it all off!

What's more, I'm sure that if God did as we pleased, it would be disastrous! He would satisfy all our whims and we would realize later on that we were mistaken. Then we'd turn to God and say, "Why did you let me do that?" So, it's better to abandon ourselves to God's will and not to want anything that he doesn't. Everything else is just pride, vanity and blindness. Now when I pray, I don't ask God for anything. What could I ask him for anyway, since I'm blind and I don't know what's good and what's bad? What's good today could be bad tomorrow. See? Now my prayer is just five words which never change: "May your will be done". Thank God...Thank you, God!

At first I wasn't very good at recognizing Godwinks. I thought that God was only in sacred things, that you could only see him in such places, like at church on Sundays. But it's not like that at all! God is everywhere, and for the simple reason that he's the one who made the entire world. He is in the flowing stream, the singing bird, the sweat of man and the giving heart. Even little nothings are divine when done with the enthusiasm of the spirit. For example, the sandwiches that mum makes me aren't just bread with ham in the middle. She puts tenderness in them, 'cause she knows that her little darling will be really happy to bite into the sandwich when she's hungry. That's why the sandwich is divine! It's a ham and God sandwich!

So God is responsible for all of Creation. He's even called the Great Architect. Which just goes to show that he's really someone! What's more, if you're not happy, all you have to do is say, "Get me the owner!" God will be there in a split second and ask, "What's the problem?"

God would like everyone to be happy on man's earth. It's just that when things aren't going well, people don't dare call for him. They think God's got better things to do. But they're wrong! His greatest pleasure is to be there when you need him, to always answer "present", but only if you call him, because, as I already said, he doesn't want to force his way into your life. So, make him happy, ask him a favour! I do all the time. I invite him into my inner sanctum. As soon as he's in... hup! I close the drawbridge and we talk, just the two of us. He gives me advice on how to cultivate my private garden, he tells me what to do so that my flowers blossom and my trees bear lots of fruit and their roots go deep. Sometimes he's a little hard to get, you have to wait twenty-four, forty-eight hours, but he never fails to come. He doesn't always have a ready answer and he doesn't try to be smart. He doesn't answer with answers, but with questions. He never says, "Do this, do that".

He takes the voice of your conscience to say,

"Don't you think that..." That way, you feel like you're free while you're really doing God's will.

God is like a dad. He seems a little severe and hard to approach, you always feel he has something else to do, something serious and important, and then you notice that he's all tender inside, and even if he doesn't really want to show it, he's all proud that we're his children.

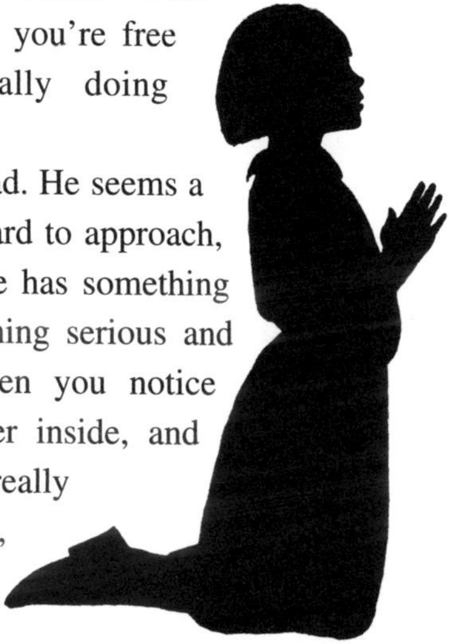

13.

What's Important for the Future of Humanity

God is smart! He has put a small piece of himself in each one of us to make sure that we don't forget him. One day Raff told me about a kind of statue that we all have inside of us.

"There are little bits of God, fragments of eternity and samplings of truth. Here and there, here and now, everywhere and always. All is present, and yet all remains to be done. It's as if God were to deliver you a block of marble. He has given you enough freedom, talent and spirit so that you decide to do something with it. If possible something of beauty, a statue, for example. But if you think about it, the statue which is going to be created by your hands and by your implements, will not really habe been created by you. It was already contained in the block of marble. You made it spring forth from the matter, you revealed it. If God hadn't given you the matter and the spirit, he wouldn't have given you the chance to create the statue.

"Now imagine that this block of marble is your life. God has given you enough freedom, talent and spirit for you to do something with it, and if possible something successful, a happy destiny, for example. But if you think about it, the destiny that will come of your efforts and your movements will not have been created by you. It was already contained in your life. You made it spring forth, you revealed it. If God had not given you a body and a spirit, he would not have given you the opportunity to live your life."

I've thought about that a lot. We have to carve out our lives, give them a form, let time do its share, in short, transform the raw stone and polish it to make something which resembles a sculpture.

Some days I think I'm Michelangelo…

There are some things I just don't get. People are always talking about peace and they never stop making war. The more they have to be happy, the less happy they are. It's kind of strange, don't you think? It all beyond me! One time I talked about this problem to Brother Michael who is an ambassador of God. When he talks, it's not all that preachy stuff. His words take off and carry your soul to the heavens. When he gives *Carpe Diem-Alleluia-Eureka* sermons, he is so celestial and he gives people such goose bumps that at the end of the service they give him a standing ovation.

The other day he gave a sermon with all sorts of gestures and then he pointed his finger towards the sky and everyone was petrified by the divine. He said: "Instead of thinking about conquering the world, man would be better off conquering his inner kingdom! You must learn to put a little order into your private gardens, by pulling out the weeds of irresolution, selfishness, greed and pride and by better cultivating the seeds of certainty, joy and sharing.

"My dear parishioners... a little girl came to see me this week and I was able to observe that the infant morality rate is clearly on the upswing! It is perhaps that children are beginning to resemble a little less the times and a little more God. They are the seeds of the future which you must learn to cultivate, because they grow into marvellous flowers, and it is quite possible that there is nothing more important for the future of humanity!"

I thought Brother Michael was exaggerating a little, and then I blushed some, because, well, I knew who the little girl was! Afterwards I went to see him and asked:

'What good is praying if you do it all alone while others just think about making war? Do you think that a little thing like me can change the future of humanity?'

'Wholeheartedly, Jade, yes I do! To start

with, you're not all alone in your prayers. There are thousands and thousands of people, maybe even millions, who are praying the world over at this very moment. It's what we call communion. You can't see it, but God can.'

'How can he see it?'

'When you look at the moon or a star, there just might be another little girl whom you don't know, on the other side of the world, looking at the same time. God sees things from above and so he can see everything at once, you Jade and the little girl on the other side of the world. Do you understand?'

'But if he's so high up, how can he see us among the thousands and thousands?'

'Listen...try to imagine that when you pray you become a light on earth. So there are as many lights as there are people who pray. And thanks to God, Mr. Holy Spirit and the help of all the saints, the sky reflects this light and illuminates the world. And that's what makes the world go round. If nobody prayed, there would be no light, and the whole world would sink into obscurity, chaos and shadows. That's why your prayer is important, Jade, because even if you were the only person to pray, even if there were only one light which stayed on, that light would be enough to save the world!'

I like to listen to Brother Michael, because he's a visionary and his vision helps me to see! Still, what he said frightened me a little, 'cause maybe one night I had almost forgotten to pray, and if I had, the whole world could have fallen into complete darkness! I didn't think I was such an important person! But then Brother Michael told me that you don't only pray with words, but also by spreading love all around, everyday, like when you light up a dark room. So you have to be illuminated within to light up without.

Sometimes Brother Michael gives people a big kick in the behind of their conscience, but he has so much love in his eyes that all the lady parishioners are crazy in love with him. Maybe that's why all the boys I know want to be priests when they grow up.

One day I asked him:

'Brother Michael, what's love?'

'It's the desire to give pleasure just for the pleasure of giving pleasure.'

'*Gratis pro Deo?*' I asked.

'Bravo! That's exactly right! For the love of God. What you must love in others is not their reflection, nor yours, but God's reflection.'

'And can you be in love with God, do you think? It's not a sin?'

'No! It's not only the opposite of sin, it's saintliness!'

'And are you very, very happy when you love very very much?'

'Of course! You know that.'

'Yea, but there are people who say, "I can't be happy if the people I love are unhappy" .

'Well, that just makes one more unhappy person! And do you think that one more unhappy person makes happiness? It doesn't make anybody happy. Everyone just waits in his corner for someone else to decide to set the example by being happy!'

'So what should you do?'

'To love is not to want to make the other person happy. It's to be happy and to offer your happiness to the other person.'

'I'm beginning to understand', I said.

In reality, I didn't understand very well. After thinking about it I told myself that to love must have something to do with *Carpe Diem-Alleluia-Eureka.*

Brother Michael kind of impresses me, because when he looks at something, it's like he sees right through it. He's used to deciphering the invisible, so in a flash he reads your sentimental topography, as if your eyes were a geography map, or else a book of short stories or a weather report that tells what the weather's like inside. For example, I'm sure that he guessed that I'm in love with God. And he doesn't only decipher the invisible, but also Greek, Latin and Hebrew, and that's really bothersome because all my secrets with Raff, nothing doing!.. He understands everything.

Brother Michael has a whole lot of pals with weird names like Plato, Aristotle, Plutarch, Epictetus and so on. I remember the last one, because he's the one who apparently once said, "Men make themselves unhappy, not because of what happens, but because of how they see what happens". I thought about my dark grey clouds and I told Brother Michael that I'd like to meet Epictetus, just to chat with him a bit. He burst out laughing and told me that such a meeting would be quite simply impossible.

'Why isn't it possible? Do you think I'm too young?'

He kept on laughing. 'No, it's more like he's too old!'

'Oh!... How old is he?'

'About two thousand years old!'

'So what? I know an old master who's one hundred and eight and we're really good friends!'

'That may be so, Jade, but Epictetus has been dead for a long time.'

'Oh! ... So I have to wait to go to the other side of life to meet him?'

'That's right. Maybe even…'

'Too bad! I had a lot of things to say to him. I hope I'll remember them later on.'

I asked Brother Michael why he hung around with guys who had been dead for so long? He told me that it was because they had a lot more to say than those who were still living.

'Cause of their wisdom?'

'No doubt, but especially because, thanks to them, we can collect fragments of eternity.'

'What are those?'

He gave me one of those smiles that makes all the lady parishioners who are crazy in love with him go into a swoon.

'It's a little like a puzzle, you see. You have little pieces spread out everywhere and you have to try and find a coherent whole. You put little pieces of truth together one next to the other. It's my favorite hobby.'

'And what's the final picture when the puzzle is finished?'

'That, I don't know yet. What do you think?'

'I have a sneaky feeling that it might just be the image of God... right?'

14.
A Little Like a Prayer

I've already had reason to question my existence. Hey, it's not the end of the world! One day, you take off on a solo voyage of inner discovery. It's a sacred experience, yea, a devilishly sacred experience! Brother Michael often repeats what one of his Greek pals used to say: "My God, give me the courage to change the things I can change, the serenity to accept the things I cannot change, and the wisdom to tell the difference".

It's the great crossing of the desert. When

above your head and all around there are thousands and thousands of stars, when silence gives you a big eternal kiss in the nape of the neck, well, I swear, you have a bodyquake, an invisible upheaval which jumbles your ideas. Afterwards you find them so tangled up that you have to pan them to separate the dirt from the gold dust. When you've been shaken around like that, there's no doubt that you're capable of transforming nuggets of enchantment into twenty-four carat ideas. *Carpe Diem-Alleluia-Eureka*!

God has a whole bunch of sesames up his sleeve, even more than Ali-Baba. He can say at any time, "Man, open yourself!", and man opens his heart, because that's the place God says to meet when he wants to visit someone.

I was so happy this morning that I wanted to take the whole world into my little arms and kiss it all over and hug it with my big tender sun just like mum does when I'm sad. Then maybe the world would be a better place. There would be no more dark grey clouds above, nothing but blue sky as far as the eye can see, as far as infinity! Maybe people would smile more because they'd feel loved. Life would really be neat then, don't you think?! We'd invite Mr. Holy Spirit to toast life, love and eternity! We'd hear songs rise in the night and soar on the wind. Amorgen would teach people about the fullness of the moment. Brother Michael wouldn't be able to get over seeing millions and millions of stars climb up towards the heavens. And Raff would have lots of clients, the "*Spirit of Wonder*" would be the mascot of the new era! Yea! Everyone would rediscover the Spirit of Wonder... That would be one great day all right!

When you're overflowing with happiness, you want to make others happy and you love them so much that you want to hold them really really tight against you, and then even tighter, like you were a small part of them and they were a small part of you. You know, I didn't really understand, but Raff even told me that it is this miracle of hearts which makes it possible to have children.

This morning, life seemed so full of flavour and juice and *fruitisity* that I wanted to bite right into it with all my teeth. So very, very much that it made my eyes shine.

I thought about the story of Fred and his apple. "All the mysteries of life are in your eyes. You simply have to train them to see beyond appearances". Well, this morning the world was overflowing with light. It got so transparent that you could see right through it, beyond appearances! I had the impression that an invisible hand was caressing the landscape and everything was more beautiful. Each thing, each bird, each tree, each leaf, each ant, everything became more beautiful for feeling loved. You know, you do get more beautiful when you feel loved... just look at flowers in the morning, how they open when the sun caresses them. They become more beautiful for having welcomed beauty. It's like they'd been touched by the hand of God.

I felt so good in all this light that I discovered the joy of breathing as if for the first time. It was as if I were inhaling a little of God's smoke with each breath. I would have liked to have gone up in smoke too, to be even lighter and become a part of the air we breathe. It would be good If I could evaporate, pfft! just like that, into infinity... I'd have a good old time like Mr. Holy

Spirit… I'd be everywhere and nowhere, and nobody would know, nobody but God. I'd turn into a smile and go fix myself on a sad person's lips. I'd turn into a laugh and go break out in the middle of a gathering of friends. I'd turn into the flavour of a kiss and go and hide in lover's hearts. I'd go see complicated people, climb a ladder up to the third floor of their subconscience and whisper to them, "Take advantage of life! It's too short to live halfway… It's today that you must be happy…Here and now! *Carpe Diem! Carpe Diem…*" And that would echo in their head, again and again. And I'd unbolt the doors for them and help them to *delabyrinthate* so that they wouldn't get shut up inside themselves. I'd shake awake the little man or the little woman who sleeps deep down inside them. I'd teach them to forget the problems they invent. I'd oblige them to look at the light so as not to feel all alone in the dark. I'd…

I'll make their eyes shine, yes I will!.. They'll want to bite into life like an apple, but first they'll have to climb to the top of the mountain, like Fred, to deserve it, to deserve all the flavour. I'll teach them to think so hard about God that each action will be a prayer. And since God likes to be convinced by prayers, everyone will be happy. It'll make Him want to miracle-make more often!

...Jade, don't you think you're going a little far? You wouldn't be mistaking yourself for the good Lord, by any chance?

At that thought I blushed, because, I must admit, I was mistaking myself for the good Lord... But I think he'll forgive me for having wanted to take his place. After all, I'm just a little thing, so my sin is in proportion. It's nothing but a tiny little sin. I need my God to love me very, very much, even if I know that God belongs to everybody. So what! I still pretend that he's all mine, as if he had a weak spot for Jade, more so than for all the billions of human beings and blades of grass. Anyhow, God doesn't make 'em like me every day, you know! It requires a lot of work, and so afterwards he takes a break. He puts a little flirtatiousness here and a little mischief there, a little sensitivity everywhere, happiness at altitude and mystery deep down. When he puts all that in the same person, the result is a bubbly, fruity and fortifying drink

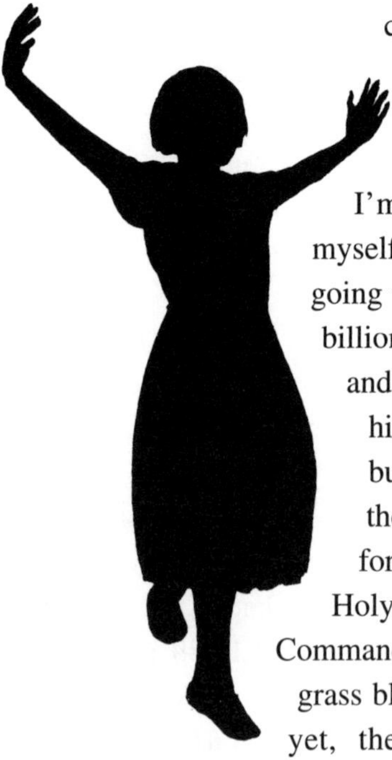

called a Jade cocktail!

So, to get pardoned for wanting to take God's place, I'm going to make myself all small-small. I'm going to hide among all the billions of blades of grass and I'm going to pray to him, not with words, but with the music of the wind and all the force from within. Mr. Holy Spirit will be the Commander in Chief of the grass blades army! Or better yet, the conductor of the grass blades symphony! And in the evening breeze, at sundown, all of the blades of grass will fall into tune with God, and the result will be such a harmonious, beautiful and delicious hymn that God will have shivers up and down his spine and yes… maybe he'll even cry.

Last night before going to sleep I said to God, "May your will be done", and then I thought that there might be a prettier way to say it, 'cause deep down, only God can save the essence of the world… I thought about it, and then I said, "May your will be fun!" And you know what? He smiled and I swear… He gave me a great big Godwink!

Contents

Excerpts

■ Intimate God – Universal God

19. God makes me so happy that sometimes I would like to have him all to myself, like a fiancé. But I can't understand that he doesn't belong to anybody but to everybody. He's both public and private, impersonal and intimate, invisible and present.

22. God… it's difficult to explain… He doesn't look like anybody you know, you don't hear him with your ears and you don't see him with your eyes. You feel him, that's all.

70. When you love someone, that someone is like God. It's someone who doesn't resemble anyone, who doesn't need to talk to be present, who is capable of lighting up the universe with a smile and, when you think hard about him, of transporting you into a world which doesn't exist or that only exists elsewhere.

■ The Presence of God and Holy Spirit

83. When there is enthusiasm, hope, joie de vivre, fraternity, prayer, you can be sure that Mr. Holy Spirit is somewhere nearby!

97. God is like a dad. He seems a little severe and hard to approach, you always feel he has something else to do, something serious and important, and then you notice that he's all tender inside, and even if he doesn't really want to show it, he's all proud that we're his children.

98. God is smart! He has put a small piece of himself in each one of us to make sure that we don't forget him.

109. God has a whole bunch of sesames up his sleeve, even more than Ali Baba. He can say at any time, "Man, open yourself!", and man open his heart, because that's the place God says to meet when he wants to visit someone.

■ Visible World– Invisible World

20. Maybe the invisible world is even truer and more beautiful than the visible one! But how can you find out? Sometimes I want to go through the drawers in my head to see if they contain any important messages, sort through them and keep only what is essential, clear them out to make more space for God, so that I can fill myself with him!

22. This Holy Spirit is like a lamplighter who lights up everything he comes near. It's easy to recognize his presence, because you breathe in a feeling of harmony, equilibrium and transparence just like a perfume. It's simple, a partnership between your little seed of life and the great garden of the infinite, between the visible and the invisible.

42. When we're surfing on a sea of mystery, we have to learn to abandon ourselves to the rhythm of the wave. It's the only way to keep our balance and not get tumbled over and our nose ground into the beach!

89. The mystery of life is in your eyes. You simply need to train them to look beyond appearances. And remember this well, that when the universe seems to darken before you, it is not because the doors are closing, but because your eyes are fleeing the light.
93. We only see the present and visible world. The future and the invisible world escape our perception.

■ Joy of Man – Joy of God

23. God's advantage is that he can make joy out of anything, even pain and suffering.
26. Our spirits remain high if they are turned upwards, towards the good Lord. If we are able to concentrate on the upside of the inside, we will never be turned inside out or upside down. Get it?
34. "What good is too much wisdom", he thought, "if it only leads to worries about tomorrow and perpetual fear of untoward happenings? Perhaps the best things in life come to an end, but they have a beginning too. So let's start to be happy."
91. As for the sun, don't worry, God knows what he's doing!
91. God is everywhere where there's light.
110. This morning life seemed so full of flavour and juice and *fruitisity* that I want to bite right into it with all my teeth. So very, very much that it made my eyes shine.

■ Man's Will – God's Will

38. What's important in life is not will, but abandon… It's simple. Rather than counting on my little personal will, I rely on God's will. I noticed that he does things much better than I can.

42. Abandon brings abundance, perpetual abundance… Where there's abandon, there's love and where there's love, there's God.

73. It isn't us or our will power that make things happen, it's our state of mind or, if you prefer, the ease with which we communicate with Mr. Holy Spirit.

115. May your will be fun!

■ Faith: The Source and the Flame

13. She said she wanted to be, not a woman, but a flame.

14. She was speaking of a flame, but not like other flames, a flame at the same time very small and fragile and that, although exposed to wind, would never go out, would not stop dancing, to give warmth, light and joy to all those that came near.

39. So long as you don't have God within, you are like an empty shell, all alone, completely alone.

43. Let God flow within you like a river. That's all. When you've understood, you'll see, life just flows naturally along…

83. God is the light, man is the candle and Mr. Holy Spirit is the wick.

■ Knowing How to Live

14. Her rule of savoir-vivre is not to avoid putting one's elbows on the table. It is to learn to stand straight. Understand: a straight spirit. To be fully worthy to take part in the feast of life.

25. One person is a little like a landscape. If you really love him, you shouldn't expect him to be always at his best.
44. Living isn't just breathing, moving, getting up, working and going to the bank to get money! Do you think that you'll remember all that at the end of your life?
45. You say, "I'll do it later". But what does "later" mean? You really want me to tell you? Later means never!
64. Live fully your joys and bravely endure your hardships.
64. Don't be so foolish as to want to resemble those around you !
87. I'd like to know what you think about before dying, because if you could know that when you're born, maybe you'd live differently!

■ Loving in Honest Truth

33. If you shut yourself in at home for fear of the rain, then the seasons will monotonously pass by and you will take shelter from the most wonderful offerings of nature, which, in the human soul, are called passions.
38. Life is a great love story and people miss out because they don't love enough.
69. True love is when silence is no longer a void to be filled, but a harmony to be shared.
103. 'What's love?'
'It's the desire to give pleasure just for the pleasure of giving pleasure…'
103. What you must love in others is not their reflec-

tion, nor yours, but God's reflection.
104. To love is not to want to make the other person happy. It's to be happy and to offer your happiness to the other person.

■ Fervour to Do and Daring to Live

12. One of Jade's discoveries that dreams only get worn out if you don't use them.
13. Our dreams must be acted upon here and now. One must taste them with eyes that shine as children's eyes shine who discover a long-awaited and desired present.
46. Do you know why people don't dare? It's because they've reduced their lives to a trickle of water. They're afraid of failing and so they open the tap slowly… drip drip drip. They're saving up, you see!
63. There are those who say "What's the use?" and who only see the obstacles to overcome, and then there are those who say "Why not?" and who only see the goal to attain.

■ The Pleasurable Consciousness of Living

56. Remember this well: you don't have time to waste your time. Life is too short to live it halfway. You must live the hours of your existence to their fullest extent. They won't all be intense, of course, because life is made of contrasts, but you can't deny any of them.
57. Each day you live eighty-six thousand four hundred seconds, do you realize? That's a hell of a stockpile, eh? You can do thousands of things in that kind of time!
58. Even when you think you're being daring, you're

not being daring enough. Remember that when you give of yourself, it's never "too much", it's always "not enough". You can never love too much. You can make a mistake, you can love badly, but you can never love enough. Never, you hear!

65. Never forget to savour the taste of life, its royal nectar gathered from flowers pure, that marvellous warm honey of secret and magic virtues.

■ The Spirit of Wonder

62. There's one quality that allows you to obtain everything and to make your dreams come true, to live a great love, never to despair, to always adore God and even to fly up into the infinite blue yonder (...) It's the most important quality in the world, the best one that a man can ever have. It's the SPIRIT OF WONDER.

89. What's important is to savour the taste of life. When you think about it, you realize what a wonderful gift it is! Really fantastic!

109. I was so happy this morning that I wanted to take the whole world into my little arms and kiss it all over and hug it with my big tender sun, just like mum does when I'm sad.

■ The Sense of Life

45. There's what you want to have, but then that's your business. What's much more interesting is what you want to *be*.

53. That is man's freedom, the power to say yes or no, to tend or to ignore, to bring to fruition or to trample underfoot.

57. The meaning of life? Here's the secret. Do your best, then let God do the rest.
75/76. Meditate the night, meditate the silence and the wind, meditate the fullness of the moment…
112. I'll teach them to think so hard about God that each action will be a prayer.

■ The Happiness of Being

66. There are three Be-Attitudes. Be beautiful, be kind and be good.
68. The first rule of happiness is always to have a smile. Well, Raff and I decided to go on good mood diets.
88. To feel good, you have to gain altitude.
99/100. People are always talking about peace and they never stop making war. The more they have to be happy, the less happy they are. It's kind of strange, don't you think?
111. I felt so good in all this light that I discovered the joy of breathing as if for the first time.

■ The Sublime Giving, Nobility of Heart and Inner Treasure…

45. If you want to do it and you don't, what good is it to be able to do it? You're no better off than the guy who can't do it! You're even worse off, because it's not the fault of the guy who can't do it, but you, you're wasting your talent.
48. The more you do for free, the richer you get.
48. Sure, you can do things for your own pleasure, but the greatest pleasure comes from giving pleasure. For

the pleasure of God! *Gratis pro Deo*!
48. Feelings that you don't give are lost feelings!
49. It would be great to be a billionaire in feelings!!
87. The moments that have counted the most, those that have echoed for the longest inside us, will be those that happened by accident and not those that we willed. It'll be those moments that filtered into our existence like water into the earth to fertilize our little seed of life. That's when we opened up, bloomed, flowered and bore fruit.

■ The Inward Paths

68. Maybe we dress reality with words because we are afraid to see it naked. Maybe we should also keep quiet more often. Learn to contemplate. Say nothing. Remain silent.
92. It is with your eyes that you perceive the light from without, and it is with your eyes that you express the light from within. Have you noticed, it's with your eyes that you give and you receive.
93. Hidden truths don't exist. Truths don't hide. It is our strange blindness that prevents us from perceiving them.
103. You don't only pray with words, but also by spreading love all around, everyday, like when you light up a dark room. So you have to be illuminated within to light up without.

The original french version is available online: www.montecristo-editions.com

ÉDITIONS MONTE-CRISTO

MONTE-CRISTO

ET SI L'ON PARLAIT
DU SENS DE LA VIE...

www.montecristo-editions.com

PRINTED IN FRANCE BY DARANTIERE, DIJON, BURGUNDY
PRINTING NUMBER 29-0459